Pharaoh's Treasure

By Amanda Brandon

Illustrated by
Michelle Simpson

Amon peered into the tent. The workers were digging for Pharaoh's treasure and the tent was where they kept the things they dug up. Amon couldn't resist a peek!

BRENT LIBRARIES

'Pharaoh's Treasure'
An original concept by Amanda Brandon
© Amanda Brandon 2022

Illustrated by Michelle Simpson

Published by MAVERICK ARTS PUBLISHING LTD
Studio 11, City Business Centre, 6 Brighton Road,
Horsham, West Sussex, RH13 5BB
© Maverick Arts Publishing Limited August 2022
+44 (0)1403 256941

A CIP catalogue record for this book is available at the British Library.
Inspired by true events

ISBN 978-1-84886-906-6

www.maverickbooks.co.uk

Purple

This book is rated as: Purple Band (Guided Reading)

On a table were some dusty pots and broken pieces of pottery. Amon looked at the strange writing on a pot and wondered who once used it. Could it have been a village boy like him? Or perhaps it had been a pharaoh? He wished he could discover objects like these too.

Suddenly, the tent flap opened. Amon dived under the table, but it was too late. He'd been spotted by Horus, the man in charge of the dig. "What are you doing here?" Horus frowned and checked everything was in order.

Amon gulped. "I was only looking," he stuttered. "I just wanted to see what had been found. A pharaoh may have drunk from that pot thousands of years ago and it hasn't been touched since. It's incredible."

Horus's frown changed to a smile.

"Ah, I see you have the treasure hunting bug. You're right, these finds are amazing. But we're still searching for one pharaoh's precious tomb and the mystery of his lost treasure."

"May I look too?" Amon's eyes gleamed. "It's exciting to discover how people used to live years ago. Their secrets are buried beneath all that sand out there."

He gave Horus a hopeful look.

Horus grinned. "Very well. I will show you how to dig. It's important to check every scoop and scrape for objects."

Amon couldn't wait.

The next morning, Horus showed him how to use

the digging tools to scoop and sift the sand.

Amon cheered when he found a fragment of an

urn. Horus noted when and where he found it.

Amon was eager to return to the dig again.

What else would he discover?

11

One afternoon, a storm swept across the valley. The sky darkened and there was a roar as the sand whipped up. It stung Amon's eyes and filled his ears. He dived for cover and the workers were forced to stop.

When the storm finished, they restarted the digging. Several days passed and nothing more was found.

"It usually takes a while," Horus told him. "Sand builds up over the years, so who knows how deep we will have to go. We need to be patient."

Amon sighed. He began to lose hope that they would ever find the Pharaoh's tomb.

One afternoon, when the sun was at its hottest,
Amon decided to rest. He sat next to a
half-buried rock.

He brushed away some sand but, suddenly,

he found something unexpected – a step!

Amon brushed away more sand and found

another step. "Over here. Over here!" he

cried in excitement.

Horus rushed over to see. He called others to help dig. Slowly, they uncovered a small stone stairway. Amon followed Horus down the steps.

It was amazing to think that they were walking where no human feet had walked for thousands of years.

Finally, they stopped in front of a small doorway. It had strange markings which Amon couldn't understand. His heart skipped a beat as he reached out and brushed his fingers on the cold stone.

Horus was amazed as he looked at the markings.

"It's a royal seal," he gasped.

Amon's eyes shone. At last! Could this be the

Pharaoh's tomb?

Amon's heart thumped as he held the flickering lamp. Horus made a hole in the door. It was just big enough for Amon to wriggle through.

Everyone was silent as he squeezed in.

He held up the lamp. Dark shadows leapt on the walls around him.

"What can you see?" Horus asked.

Amon's eyes sparkled at the glittering gold all around him. "It's treasure!" he replied.

Horus called for some workers to make the hole bigger and they crawled into the tomb.

In the lamplight, they were dazzled by the sight in front of them. The tomb was filled with jewellery, chariots, paintings and statues.

Horus clasped Amon's hands and spun him around.

"We did it!" he beamed.

One room contained objects for the Pharaoh to use in the afterlife. Amon saw that there were eating and cooking tools and even some clothing. He sniffed. He was sure he could smell perfume in the air too.

Then, Amon rubbed his eyes in disbelief.

In front of him was a door guarded by two

tall statues of a pharaoh. The workers carefully

opened it and discovered the Pharaoh's burial

chamber – and even more riches.

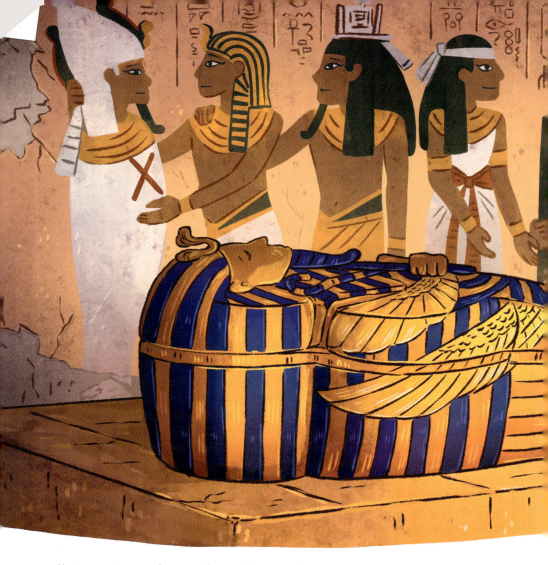

"Wow! Look at the Pharaoh's golden mask,"
Amon gasped. "We're the first people to see this
for thousands of years," Amon's voice dropped
to a whisper as he marvelled at all the finds.

"Just think how many other wonders from the past are waiting to be discovered," Amon said. "I'm never going to stop looking!"

Quiz

1. Who was in charge of the dig?
a) Horus
b) Amon
c) Seth

2. What did Amon find on his first dig with Horus?
a) A fragment of an urn
b) A necklace
c) A ring

3. Why did the dig have to stop?
a) It was too hot
b) The workers were hungry
c) There was a storm

4. What did Amon find next to a half-buried rock?

a) Treasure

b) Steps

c) A trap door

5. What colour is the Pharaoh's mask?

a) Purple

b) Blue

c) Gold

Turn over for answers

Book Bands for Guided Reading

The Institute of Education book banding system is a scale of colours that reflects the various levels of reading difficulty. The bands are assigned by taking into account the content, the language style, the layout and phonics. Word, phrase and sentence level work is also taken into consideration.

Maverick Early Readers are a bright, attractive range of books covering the pink to white bands. All of these books have been book banded for guided reading to the industry standard and edited by a leading educational consultant.

To view the whole Maverick Readers scheme, visit our website at www.maverickearlyreaders.com

Or scan the QR code above to view our scheme instantly!

Quiz Answers: 1a, 2a, 3c, 4b, 5c